THE FLUFFY WORLD OF PANCAKE

SHAIKH ABDULAZIZ

Made with ♥ on the Notion Press Platform
www.notionpress.com

Contents

Dedication

This fluffy and delicious stack of goodness is for you. May your mornings be filled with the sweet aroma of freshly made pancakes and your plates be piled high with your favorite toppings. May you always remember to flip with confidence and never let a pancake go unflipped. Here's to the simple joy of pancakes, a beloved breakfast classic that will always hold a special place in our hearts (and stomachs).

pancakes are a beloved breakfast food enjoyed by people all over the world. The dedication of pancakes can be seen in the various ways they are prepared, served, and enjoyed.

Firstly, the preparation of pancakes requires patience and skill. The batter must be mixed just right to achieve the perfect consistency, and then carefully poured onto a hot griddle or frying pan. The cook must watch the pancakes closely to ensure they are cooked evenly on both sides, and flip them at just the right moment to achieve a perfect golden brown color.

Secondly, the serving of pancakes is often a ritualistic affair. Some people prefer them stacked high, others prefer them spread out flat on a plate. They can be topped with a variety of sweet or savory ingredients, such as maple syrup, butter, whipped cream, fruit, bacon, or eggs.

Lastly, the enjoyment of pancakes is a communal experience. Many families gather around the breakfast table on weekend mornings to enjoy a hearty meal of pancakes together. In some cultures, pancakes are even associated with religious or cultural celebrations, such as Mardi Gras or Shrove Tuesday.

Overall, the dedication of pancakes can be seen in the way they are prepared, served, and enjoyed by people of all ages and backgrounds. They are a simple yet satisfying breakfast food that brings people together and adds a touch of warmth and comfort to the start of each day.

Foreword

I am the co-author writing about the Forward section of this book where I would like to let you know some history of PANCAKES.

Let's go back to ancient Greece and Rome. Yes, you read that right! In ancient Greece and Rome, pancakes were made from wheat flour, olive oil, honey, and curdled milk. In fact, Cratinus and Magnes, Ancient Greek poets, wrote about pancakes in their poetry. There were also references to pancakes in some of Shakespeare's famous plays. During the English Renaissance, pancakes were often flavored with rosewater, various spices, sherry, and apples.

The name "pancake" became a standard name in the 19th century in America. Before that, they were often referenced as johnnycakes, journey cakes, buckwheat cakes, hoe cakes, griddle cakes, and flapjacks. Most early American pancakes were made with buckwheat or cornmeal.

The interesting fact about pancakes is that they exist all throughout the world, but each culture has their own unique way of preparing them for breakfast, lunch, and dinner. Take for example these extensions of transcultural food: Crêpes, Irish boxty, Welsh crampog, potato latkes, Indian poori, Hungarian palacsinta, Russian blini, and Dutch pannenkoeken.

So whether you prefer the classic pancake for breakfast, potato cakes for lunch, chicken and waffles for dinner, or like to try unique flavor combinations, this tasty, easy-to-make treat is sure to please everyone at the kitchen table.

Pancakes are a delicious and versatile food that have been enjoyed by people for centuries. They are a type of flat, round cake made from a batter of flour, eggs, milk, and other ingredients, such as sugar, baking powder, and butter. Pancakes are often served for breakfast, but they can be enjoyed at any time of day and can be prepared in a variety of ways to suit different tastes and dietary requirements.

Pancakes have a long history, dating back to ancient civilizations such as the Greeks and Romans, who made a form of pancake called "alita docia" with wheat flour, olive oil, honey, and milk. Pancakes are now a popular food all around the world, with many different variations and regional specialties. Whether you like your pancakes sweet or savory, thin or thick, plain or loaded with toppings, there is a pancake recipe out there for everyone.

Preface

Pancakes are a type of flat cake made from a simple batter of flour, eggs, milk, and usually baking powder or baking soda to create a light, fluffy texture. Pancakes are a popular breakfast food in many parts of the world and are often served with butter and syrup or other sweet or savory toppings.

Pancakes have a long history, dating back to ancient civilizations such as the Greeks and Romans who made similar flat cakes. The modern version of pancakes that we know today became popular in the 19th century, and the recipe has evolved over time to include a variety of different ingredients and styles.

While pancakes are often associated with breakfast, they can be enjoyed at any time of day and are a versatile food that can be customized to suit a wide range of tastes and preferences. From classic buttermilk pancakes to more unique variations like pumpkin pancakes or chocolate chip pancakes, there's a pancake recipe out there for everyone to enjoy.

A pancake (or hotcake, griddlecake, or flapjack) is a flat cake, often thin and round, prepared from a starch-based batter that may contain eggs, milk and butter and cooked on a hot surface such as a griddle or frying pan, often frying with oil or butter. It is a type of batter bread. Archaeological evidence suggests that pancakes were probably eaten in prehistoric societies.

The pancake's shape and structure varies worldwide. In the United Kingdom, pancakes are often unleavened and resemble a crêpe.[2] In North America, a leavening agent is used (typically baking powder) creating a thick fluffy pancake. A crêpe is a thin Breton pancake of French origin cooked on one or both sides in a special pan or crepe maker to achieve a lacelike network of fine bubbles. A well-known variation originating from southeast Europe is a palačinke, a thin moist pancake fried on both sides and filled with jam, cream cheese, chocolate, or ground walnuts, but many other fillings—sweet or savoury—can also be used.

Commercially prepared pancake mixes are available in some countries. Like waffles, commercially prepared frozen pancakes are available from companies like Eggo. When buttermilk is used in place of or in addition to milk, the pancake develops a tart flavor and becomes known as a buttermilk pancake, which is common in Scotland and the US. Buckwheat flour can be used in a pancake batter, making for a type of buckwheat pancake, a category that includes Blini, Kaletez, Ploye, and Memil-buchimgae. When potato is used as a major portion of the batter, the result is a potato pancake.

Pancakes may be served at any time of the day or year with a variety of toppings or fillings, but they have developed associations with particular times and toppings in different regions. In North America, they are typically considered a breakfast food and serve a similar function to waffles. In Britain and the Commonwealth, they are associated with Shrove Tuesday, commonly known as "Pancake Day", when, historically, perishable ingredients had to be used up before the fasting period of Lent.

1. The Origin of Pancakes

Pancakes have been around for centuries and are enjoyed all over the world. The ancient Greeks and Romans made pancakes as a part of their everyday diet, and it was a popular food during the Middle Ages. The word "pancake" comes from the flat, round shape of the cake and the fact that it's cooked on a pan. The origin of pancakes is not entirely clear, as pancakes have been around for centuries and were made by various cultures throughout history. However, it is known that pancakes were a popular food during the Middle Ages and were made from a mixture of flour, eggs, and milk.

The ancient Greeks and Romans also made pancakes, which they called "tiganites". These pancakes were made with wheat flour, olive oil, honey, and curdled milk. In fact, the Greeks had a whole festival dedicated to pancakes, called "Apomagia", which was celebrated in February.

In medieval Europe, pancakes were often made with buckwheat or oats and were eaten during the pre-Lenten period, known as "Shrovetide". This period was marked by feasting and the consumption of rich foods before the period of fasting and abstinence during Lent.

In America, pancakes were a staple food of the Native American tribes, who made them from cornmeal or acorns. The colonists adopted this food and made their own versions using wheat flour, eggs, and milk. Pancakes soon became a popular breakfast food in America and were often served with butter and syrup.

Today, pancakes are enjoyed all over the world and are made with a variety of ingredients and toppings, from classic butter and syrup to bacon and eggs. They continue to be a beloved comfort food that brings people together.

Pancakes are a popular breakfast food that have been enjoyed by many cultures around the world for centuries. The exact origin of pancakes is unknown, but there are several theories about how they came to be.

One theory suggests that pancakes were first made by ancient Greeks who cooked flat, round cakes called "tēganitēs" on a hot stone. These cakes were made with wheat flour, olive oil, honey, and curdled milk. They were often served with honey and sesame seeds, and were considered a luxury food in ancient Greece.

Another theory suggests that pancakes were first made in ancient Rome, where they were called "alita docia." These were sweet pancakes made with milk, eggs, and flour, and were often served with honey or fruit.

Pancakes also have a long history in English cuisine. In the Middle Ages, pancakes were made with ale, which acted as a leavening agent. These pancakes were often served on Shrove Tuesday, the day before the start of Lent, as a way to use up rich ingredients like eggs and milk before the fasting period.

In the United States, pancakes are often associated with the traditional breakfast served at diners and pancake houses. American pancakes are typically made with flour, eggs, milk, and baking powder, and are often served with butter and maple syrup.

Overall, pancakes have a rich and diverse history that spans many cultures and time periods. While the exact origin of pancakes is uncertain, they continue to be a beloved breakfast food enjoyed by people around the world.

Today's good mood is sponsored by pancakes.

2. Ingredients for the Perfect Pancake

Here are the ingredients you will need to make the perfect pancake:

- 1 cup all-purpose flour
- 2 tablespoons sugar
- 2 teaspoons baking powder
- 1/2 teaspoon baking soda
- 1/2 teaspoon salt
- 1 cup milk
- 1 large egg
- 2 tablespoons melted butter or vegetable oil
- 1 teaspoon vanilla extract (optional)

Instructions:

1. In a large bowl, whisk together the flour, sugar, baking powder, baking soda, and salt.
2. In a separate bowl, whisk together the milk, egg, melted butter or oil, and vanilla extract (if using).
3. Pour the wet ingredients into the dry ingredients and stir until just combined. Do not overmix the batter.

4. Heat a nonstick or cast iron skillet over medium heat. When the skillet is hot, ladle about 1/4 cup of batter onto the skillet for each pancake.
5. Cook the pancakes for about 2-3 minutes on the first side, or until bubbles form on the surface of the pancake and the edges start to look set.
6. Flip the pancake and cook for an additional 1-2 minutes on the second side, or until the pancake is golden brown and cooked through.
7. Serve the pancakes hot, with butter and maple syrup or your favorite toppings.

"*Enjoy your perfect pancakes!*"

The perfect pancake starts with the right ingredients. Here are the essential components for a basic pancake recipe:

Flour: All-purpose flour is commonly used for pancakes, but other flours, such as whole wheat or gluten-free, can be used for a healthier or dietary-specific option.

Baking powder: This is what makes the pancake fluffy and light.

Salt: Just a pinch of salt enhances the flavor of the pancake.

Eggs: Eggs add moisture and structure to the pancake.

Milk: Milk adds liquid to the batter and contributes to the richness of the pancake. Any type of milk, including non-dairy options like almond milk or oat milk, can be used.

Oil or butter: Oil or melted butter can be added to the batter to add moisture and enhance the flavor.

Sugar: Some recipes may call for sugar to be added to the batter to give the pancake a slightly sweet taste.

Vanilla extract: Vanilla extract can be added to the batter to give the pancake a subtle, sweet flavor.

Optional ingredients that can be added to the pancake batter for flavor and texture include cinnamon, mashed bananas, chocolate chips, blueberries, or nuts.

> *"With the right ingredients and a bit of practice, anyone can make the perfect pancake."*

Ingredients of Pan cake

3. The Art of Flipping Pancakes

Flipping pancakes is a skill that can take a bit of practice to master, but with some tips and tricks, anyone can become a pro at flipping pancakes. Here are some key things to keep in mind:

Use the right pan: A non-stick skillet or griddle is the best type of pan for flipping pancakes. Make sure the pan is heated evenly to prevent hot spots.

Oil or butter the pan: Grease the pan with a small amount of oil or butter to prevent the pancake from sticking.

Wait for the right moment: Wait until the edges of the pancake start to dry out and small bubbles form on the surface before flipping. This usually takes about 2-3 minutes.

Use a spatula: Slide a spatula under the pancake and gently lift it up. If the pancake is sticking, use a spatula to loosen it from the pan before attempting to flip.

Flip with confidence: Quickly flip the pancake over by using a flick of the wrist. Try to flip the pancake in one fluid motion, rather than hesitating or flipping too slowly.

Don't flatten the pancake: Resist the urge to press down on the pancake with the spatula after flipping. This can make the pancake dense and tough.

Practice makes perfect: Flipping pancakes takes practice, so don't get discouraged if your first few attempts aren't perfect. Keep trying and soon you'll be flipping pancakes like a pro.

Remember, flipping pancakes is an art, not a science. Experiment with different techniques and find what works best for you. With a bit of practice and patience, anyone can master the art of flipping pancakes.

Flipping pancakes is an art form that takes practice to master. It's essential to make sure the pancake is cooked on one side before attempting to flip it. Using a spatula, carefully lift the pancake from the pan and quickly flip it. The trick is to get the timing right, so the pancake lands perfectly on the other side without breaking apart.

Flipping pancakes can be both a science and an art. To achieve the perfect flip, you need to use the right technique and timing. Here are some tips for mastering the art of flipping pancakes:

Use the right pan: A non-stick or well-seasoned cast-iron pan is best for flipping pancakes. Make sure the pan is evenly heated before you start cooking.

Prepare the batter: A good pancake batter is key to a successful flip. Mix the ingredients thoroughly, but avoid over-mixing, as this can result in tough pancakes. Let the batter rest for a few minutes before cooking.Use the right technique: To flip the pancake, slide a spatula underneath it and lift it up slightly. Then, with a quick flick of the wrist, flip the pancake over. Be confident and don't hesitate, as this can cause the

pancake to break.Cook on the other side: Once you've flipped the pancake, cook it on the other side for about the same amount of time as the first side. You may need to adjust the heat of the pan to ensure the pancake doesn't burn.
Serve and enjoy: Once the pancake is cooked, transfer it to a plate and serve it with your favorite toppings, such as butter, syrup, or fruit.

> "*Remember, practice makes perfect when it comes to flipping pancakes. Don't be discouraged if your first few attempts don't turn out perfectly – keep practicing and soon you'll be flipping pancakes like a pro!*"

Just Flip it and Eat it

4. The World's Best Pancakes

Pancakes are a beloved breakfast food around the world, and each culture has its own unique take on the dish. In America, pancakes are often served with butter and syrup. In France, they are known as crepes and are filled with various sweet or savory fillings. In Japan, pancakes are called hotcakes and are often served with fruit and whipped cream.

There are many delicious pancake recipes out there, but here is a recipe for a classic American pancake that is fluffy, tender, and sure to satisfy your pancake cravings!

Instructions:

In a large mixing bowl, whisk together the flour, baking powder, salt, and sugar.

In a separate bowl, beat the egg and then stir in the milk and melted butter.

Add the wet ingredients to the dry ingredients and stir until just combined. Be careful not to overmix the batter, as this can result in tough pancakes.

Heat a non-stick griddle or frying pan over medium-high heat. Once hot, pour 1/4 cup of batter onto the griddle for each pancake.

Cook for 2-3 minutes, or until the surface of the pancake is covered with bubbles and the edges begin to dry. Flip the pancake and cook for an additional minute, or until golden brown.

Serve hot with your favorite toppings, such as maple syrup, butter, fresh fruit, whipped cream, or chocolate chips.

"*Enjoy your delicious homemade pancakes!*"

There are many different types of pancakes enjoyed around the world, each with their unique flavors and textures. Here are a few popular pancake recipes that you can try out:

American Pancakes: These fluffy, thick pancakes are a breakfast favorite in the United States. To make them, you'll need all-purpose flour, baking powder, salt, milk, eggs, butter, and sugar. Mix the dry ingredients in one bowl and the wet ingredients in another, then combine the two and cook on a griddle until golden brown.

French Crepes: These thin, delicate pancakes are a staple in French cuisine. To make them, you'll need flour, milk, eggs, sugar, vanilla, and butter. Whisk all the ingredients together in a bowl, then pour a small amount of batter onto a hot skillet and swirl it around to cover the surface. Cook until the edges start to lift, then flip and cook for another few seconds.

Japanese Souffle Pancakes: These light, airy pancakes are a popular dessert in Japan. To make them, you'll need all-purpose flour, baking powder, milk, eggs, sugar, vanilla extract, and cornstarch. Beat the egg whites until stiff peaks form, then fold in the other ingredients to create a fluffy batter. Cook on a non-stick pan or griddle over low heat, using a ring mold to help the pancakes rise.

Swedish Pancakes: These thin, crepe-like pancakes are often served with lingonberry jam and whipped cream in Sweden. To make them, you'll need flour, milk, eggs, sugar, salt, and butter. Mix the ingredients together in a blender, then cook in a hot skillet until golden brown on both sides.

No matter which type of pancake you choose to make, be sure to top them with your favorite syrup, fruit, or other toppings for a delicious and satisfying breakfast or dessert.

Delicious Pancake

5. Pancakes for All Occasions

Pancakes are versatile and can be enjoyed for any meal of the day. They can be made with a variety of toppings, from traditional butter and syrup to bacon and eggs. Pancakes are also a great dessert option and can be topped with whipped cream, fruit, or chocolate chips.

Pancakes are a delicious and versatile food that can be enjoyed on many occasions! Here are some examples:

Breakfast: Pancakes are a classic breakfast food and are often enjoyed with butter and syrup or other toppings like berries, whipped cream, and chocolate chips.

Brunch: If you're having a brunch party, pancakes can be a perfect addition to the menu. You can even make a pancake bar with different toppings and syrups to let your guests customize their own pancakes.

Shrove Tuesday (also known as Pancake Day): This is a traditional Christian holiday that falls on the day before Ash Wednesday, which marks the beginning of Lent. Pancakes are often eaten on this day as a way to use up rich ingredients like eggs, butter, and sugar before the fasting period of Lent begins.

Birthdays: Pancakes can make a fun and festive breakfast on a birthday morning. You can even stack them up and decorate them with candles for a unique and tasty birthday "cake."

Camping trips: Pancakes are a great camping food, as they are easy to make over a campfire or portable stove. They can be a hearty and satisfying breakfast to fuel up for a day of outdoor activities.

Family dinners: If you're looking for a simple and delicious meal that the whole family will enjoy, pancakes can be a great option. You can add a variety of mix-ins like bananas, blueberries, or chocolate chips to make them extra special.

Late-night snack: Sometimes you just need a sweet and satisfying snack before bed. Pancakes can be a great option, as they are quick and easy to make and can satisfy a sweet tooth.

Pancakes are a versatile and delicious food that can be enjoyed for any occasion, whether it's breakfast, lunch, dinner, or dessert. Here are some ideas for pancakes that are perfect for different occasions:

Classic Pancakes: These are the perfect breakfast pancakes that can be enjoyed with butter and maple syrup. You can also add toppings like fresh fruit, whipped cream, chocolate chips, or peanut butter.

Blueberry Pancakes: Blueberry pancakes are a breakfast classic that are perfect for a lazy Sunday morning. The fresh blueberries add a burst of sweetness and color to the pancakes.

Chocolate Chip Pancakes: Chocolate chip pancakes are perfect for a weekend brunch or a fun breakfast treat. These pancakes are a hit with kids and adults alike.

Banana Pancakes: Banana pancakes are a great way to use up ripe bananas and add natural sweetness to the pancakes. These pancakes are perfect for breakfast or as a snack.

Savory Pancakes: Savory pancakes are a great option for lunch or dinner. You can make pancakes with spinach, cheese, bacon, or other savory ingredients.

Vegan Pancakes: Vegan pancakes are a great option for those who are dairy-free or vegan. You can use ingredients like flaxseed, almond milk, or banana to make vegan pancakes that are just as tasty as traditional pancakes.

Gluten-Free Pancakes: Gluten-free pancakes are perfect for those who have a gluten intolerance or celiac disease. You can use ingredients like almond flour or coconut flour to make delicious gluten-free pancakes.

Red Velvet Pancakes: Red velvet pancakes are a fun and festive dessert option. These pancakes are perfect for Valentine's Day, Christmas, or any special occasion.

Lemon Ricotta Pancakes: Lemon ricotta pancakes are a delicious and sophisticated option for breakfast or brunch. The ricotta cheese adds a creamy texture and the lemon adds a tangy flavor.

Pumpkin Pancakes: Pumpkin pancakes are a perfect fall breakfast option. These pancakes are made with pumpkin puree and pumpkin pie spice, and are perfect with a dollop of whipped cream and a sprinkle of cinnamon.

6. Fun Pancake Shapes and Designs

"Pancake Octopus"

Making pancakes in fun shapes and designs can add a touch of creativity and excitement to your breakfast. Here are some fun pancake shapes and designs you can try:

Animal Shapes: Use a cookie cutter to create animal shapes like cats, dogs, or even dinosaurs.

Letters and Numbers: Use a squeeze bottle to spell out your name or initials with pancake batter. You can also make numbers for special occasions like birthdays or anniversaries.

Emoji Pancakes: Use a squeeze bottle to draw faces on your pancakes, like heart eyes, a smiley face, or a wink.

Pancake Stack: Create a tower of small pancakes stacked on top of each other. You can add fruit, whipped cream, or other toppings in between each pancake layer.

Rainbow Pancakes: Divide your batter into small bowls and add food coloring to each one. Cook each pancake in a different color and stack them in a rainbow pattern.

Pancake Art: Use a squeeze bottle to draw intricate designs on your pancakes, like flowers, butterflies, or abstract patterns.

Pancake Shapes: Use a mold to create fun shapes like stars, hearts, or even your favorite cartoon characters.

Pancake Faces: Use chocolate chips, fruit, or other toppings to create silly pancake faces. You can add eyes, noses, and even hair using these ingredients.

Waffle Cones: Roll up your pancakes into a cone shape and fill them with fruit, whipped cream, or other toppings.

Mini Pancake Kabobs: Cut small pancakes into bite-size pieces and thread them onto skewers with fruit, bacon, or other toppings for a fun and easy breakfast kabob.

Ingredients:

Pancake batter

Chocolate chips or blueberries

Butter

Syrup

Instructions:

Heat up a non-stick pan over medium heat.

Mix the pancake batter according to the instructions.

Use a ladle to pour the batter into the pan to form a round shape.

Use a spatula to flip the pancake over when it starts to bubble and the edges look set.

Once the pancake is cooked, transfer it to a plate.

Cut two small circles out of the pancake for eyes.

Use butter to create the pupils of the eyes by placing small dots of butter in the center of each eye.

Create eight legs by cutting the pancake with a knife into eight thin strips.
Arrange the legs around the bottom of the pancake to create the octopus shape.
Use chocolate chips or blueberries to make suction cups on the bottom of each leg.
Serve with syrup.
Enjoy your pancake octopus!
Pancakes can be made into fun shapes and designs for special occasions or just for fun. Using a cookie cutter, pancake molds, or even a steady hand and a spatula, pancakes can be made into hearts, stars, animals, or any other design you can imagine.

Design on Pancake

7. Pancake Tips and Tricks

Here are some tips and tricks for making great pancakes:

Use a non-stick pan or griddle: This will make it easier to flip the pancakes and prevent them from sticking to the pan.Preheat your pan: Make sure your pan is heated to the right temperature before you start cooking your pancakes. A medium heat is usually best for cooking pancakes.

Use a ladle or measuring cup: Use a ladle or measuring cup to pour the batter onto the pan, so that you can make evenly sized pancakes.

Let the batter rest: After mixing your batter, let it rest for a few minutes before cooking. This will allow the ingredients to blend together and create a smoother texture.Don't overmix the batter: Overmixing the batter can cause the gluten in the flour to develop, resulting in tough and rubbery pancakes. Mix just until the ingredients are combined.

Flip the pancakes once: Only flip the pancakes once to ensure that they cook evenly and don't become overcooked.

Keep the pancakes warm: Once your pancakes are cooked, place them on a baking sheet in a warm oven to keep them warm until serving.

Experiment with toppings: Pancakes can be topped with a wide variety of ingredients, such as fresh fruit, whipped cream, nuts, chocolate chips, or syrup. Don't be afraid to get creative and try new combinations!

Making the perfect pancake takes practice, but there are a few tips and tricks that can help you achieve pancake perfection. For example, preheating your pan or griddle, using a ladle to scoop the batter, and letting the pancake cook until bubbles form on the surface can all help you make the perfect pancake.

Here are some tips and tricks to make perfect pancakes:

Use a non-stick pan or griddle: This will ensure that your pancakes don't stick to the pan and will make flipping them much easier.

Use the right temperature: Set your stove or griddle to medium heat. If the heat is too high, your pancakes will cook too quickly on the outside and remain raw on the inside.

Use a batter with the right consistency: A good pancake batter should be smooth and pourable, but not too thin or too thick. If the batter is too thick, your pancakes will turn out dense, and if it's too thin, they will be too thin and fall apart.

Don't overmix the batter: Overmixing can make the pancakes tough and chewy. Mix the batter until the dry ingredients are just incorporated with the wet ingredients.

Let the batter rest: Allow the batter to rest for at least 10 minutes before cooking. This allows the gluten in the flour to relax and makes the pancakes fluffier.

Use a ladle or measuring cup to pour the batter: This will help you control the amount of batter you're using and ensure that your pancakes are all the same size.

Add some extras: You can add chocolate chips, blueberries, or bananas to your pancake batter for some extra flavor and texture.

Flip the pancake when the surface is covered in bubbles: Wait until the surface of the pancake is covered in bubbles before flipping. This will ensure that the pancake is cooked all the way through and won't fall apart when you flip it.

Keep your pancakes warm: Keep your cooked pancakes warm in a 200°F oven while you finish cooking the rest of the batch.

Serve with your favorite toppings: Butter, maple syrup, whipped cream, and fresh fruit are all great toppings for pancakes. Enjoy!

Difference of Pancake

8. Pancake Recipes

"Here's a basic pancake recipe that serves four people:"

Ingredients:

- 1 1/2 cups all-purpose flour
- 3 1/2 teaspoons baking powder
- 1 teaspoon salt
- 1 tablespoon white sugar
- 1 1/4 cups milk
- 1 egg
- 3 tablespoons butter, melted

Instructions:

In a large bowl, whisk together the flour, baking powder, salt, and sugar.

In a separate bowl, beat the egg and then add the milk and melted butter, whisking to combine.

Pour the wet ingredients into the dry ingredients and stir until just combined. Do not overmix; it's okay if there are a few lumps in the batter.

Heat a non-stick skillet or griddle over medium-high heat. Scoop 1/4 cup of batter for each pancake onto the skillet.

Cook until bubbles form on the surface of the pancake and the edges look set, then flip and cook for another 1-2 minutes or until golden brown.
Serve hot with your favorite toppings, such as maple syrup, whipped cream, or fruit.

"***Enjoy your homemade pancakes!***"

From classic buttermilk pancakes to vegan and gluten-free options, there are endless pancake recipes to choose from. This chapter will include a variety of recipes to suit every taste, including recipes for savory pancakes, pancake muffins, and even pancake sandwiches.
Sure, here are a few pancake recipes for you:

"***Classic Pancakes***"

Ingredients:

- 1 1/2 cups all-purpose flour
- 3 1/2 teaspoons baking powder
- 1 teaspoon salt
- 1 tablespoon white sugar
- 1 1/4 cups milk
- 1 egg
- 3 tablespoons butter, melted

Instructions:

In a large mixing bowl, combine the flour, baking powder, salt, and sugar.

In another bowl, beat the egg and then add the milk and melted butter.

Add the wet ingredients to the dry ingredients and mix until just combined. Don't overmix.

Heat a non-stick pan or griddle over medium-high heat. Drop spoonfuls of batter onto the pan and cook until bubbles form on the surface, then flip and cook for an additional 1-2 minutes.

Serve hot with your favorite toppings.

"***Blueberry Pancakes***"

Ingredients:

- 1 1/2 cups all-purpose flour
- 3 1/2 teaspoons baking powder
- 1 teaspoon salt
- 1 tablespoon white sugar
- 1 1/4 cups milk
- 1 egg
- 3 tablespoons butter, melted
- 1 cup fresh blueberries

Instructions:

Follow the same instructions as for the Classic Pancakes recipe, but add the blueberries to the batter after mixing the wet and dry ingredients.

Cook the pancakes as directed above, being careful not to squish the blueberries when flipping.

Serve hot with butter and maple syrup.

"Banana Pancakes"

Ingredients:

- 1 1/2 cups all-purpose flour
- 3 1/2 teaspoons baking powder
- 1 teaspoon salt
- 1 tablespoon white sugar
- 1 1/4 cups milk
- 1 egg
- 3 tablespoons butter, melted
- 1 ripe banana, mashed

Instructions:

Follow the same instructions as for the Classic Pancakes recipe, but add the mashed banana to the wet ingredients before mixing with the dry ingredients.

Cook the pancakes as directed above.

"Serve hot with sliced bananas, butter, and honey."

9. Pancake Art

Pancake art is a form of culinary art where pancake batter is used to create intricate and detailed designs on a hot griddle or pan. The designs can range from simple shapes and patterns to complex images of people, animals, and landscapes. To create pancake art, the artist typically uses a squeeze bottle or a piping bag to carefully apply the pancake batter onto the griddle in the desired shape or design. The artist must work quickly, as pancake batter can cook very fast, and must use different shades of batter to create a more detailed design.

Pancake art has gained popularity in recent years, with many professional and amateur chefs showcasing their creations on social media platforms. Some restaurants and cafes even offer pancake art as a menu item, with customers able to choose from a selection of pre-made designs or even request a custom design.

Overall, pancake art is a fun and creative way to enjoy breakfast and showcase culinary skills.

Pancake art is a unique form of food art that involves creating intricate designs and images using pancake batter. This chapter will explore the world of pancake art and provide tips and tricks for creating your own pancake masterpieces. Pancake art is a form of culinary art in which pancake batter is used to create images, designs, and patterns on a griddle or frying pan. The technique involves using different colored batters, as well as various tools and utensils, to create intricate designs.

To create pancake art, the pancake batter is first mixed with food coloring to create different colors. The batter is then poured onto a hot griddle or frying pan in a specific pattern, and cooked until the pancake is set. The design can be enhanced by using additional batter to create different shades and highlights.

Pancake art has become a popular trend in recent years, with many restaurants and cafes specializing in pancake art. There are even pancake art competitions and championships held around the world, where contestants create intricate and detailed designs. Pancake art is a fun and creative way to make breakfast more exciting and appealing. It's also a great activity for kids to try, as it allows them to explore their creativity in the kitchen.

Pancake art is the practice of creating artistic designs using pancake batter as a medium. It has become increasingly popular in recent years, with many professional and amateur chefs creating intricate designs using pancake batter. The process typically involves preparing a pancake batter, then using a squeeze bottle or similar tool to carefully dispense the batter onto a hot griddle or frying pan in order to create various shapes and designs. Once the pancake has cooked on one side, the artist can flip it over to cook the other side and complete the design.

Some pancake artists use food coloring to create vibrant colors and enhance the visual appeal of their designs. Popular designs include animals, cartoon characters, and other recognizable figures, but artists are free to create whatever they can imagine.

Pancake art can be a fun and creative way to express oneself in the kitchen, and it has even been featured in cooking competitions and on television shows. It can be enjoyed as a family activity or as a way to impress guests with a unique and visually appealing breakfast.

Art on Pan cake

10. The Future of Pancakes

The future of pancake is likely to see continued innovation and creativity in terms of both flavor and presentation. Some possible trends for the future of pancake include:

Healthier options: With an increasing focus on health and wellness, we may see more pancake recipes that incorporate alternative flours, such as coconut or almond flour, and use natural sweeteners like honey or maple syrup instead of refined sugar. Vegan and gluten-free options: As more people adopt plant-based or gluten-free diets, we may see more pancake recipes that cater to these dietary restrictions.

Fusion flavors: Pancakes have traditionally been associated with sweet flavors, but there is potential to experiment with savory flavors as well. We may see more pancake recipes that incorporate global flavors and ingredients, such as Japanese-style matcha pancakes or Mexican-inspired cornmeal pancakes.

Technology integration: With the advent of 3D printing and other advanced kitchen technologies, it's possible that we may see pancake art taken to the next level. Imagine a machine that can perfectly replicate any image or design you can think of in pancake form!

Overall, the future of pancake is bright and full of possibilities. Whether you prefer your pancakes classic and fluffy or avant-garde and creative, there's no doubt that pancakes will continue to be a beloved breakfast staple for years to come.

As technology advances, so does the world of pancakes. This chapter will explore the latest pancake trends, from high-tech pancake printers to virtual reality pancake experiences.

> ***"However, I can speculate on some possible trends and innovations that may shape the future of pancakes."***

Healthier options: As people become more health-conscious, there may be an increasing demand for pancakes made with alternative flours such as almond, coconut or chickpea flour. Additionally, toppings such as fresh fruits, nuts, and natural sweeteners could become more popular than the traditional butter and syrup toppings.

Plant-based pancakes: With the rise of veganism and plant-based diets, there may be more interest in pancakes made with non-dairy milk and egg substitutes, such as applesauce, bananas, or chia seeds.

Unique and unusual flavors: Pancakes have already started to expand beyond the traditional flavors, such as pumpkin spice, blueberry, or chocolate chip pancakes. In the future, we could see even more unusual and exotic flavors such as matcha, lavender, or even savory flavors like bacon and cheddar.

Technological advancements: There could be new cooking tools and gadgets that make pancake-making easier, faster and more consistent. For example, an AI-powered pancake machine that can mix and cook the perfect pancakes with just a push of a button.

Novelty shapes and designs: Pancakes could evolve from their traditional circular shape to creative and fun designs like animals, characters, or custom shapes. Pancake art could become a popular trend, where people create intricate designs with different colored batters.

Overall, while the basic recipe for pancakes may remain the same, the future of pancakes is likely to be shaped by changing consumer preferences, health concerns, and technological innovations.

Life is better with pancakes

11. Sad story of pancake

Once upon a time, there was a pancake named Patty. Patty was a beautiful pancake, round and golden brown, with a perfectly smooth surface. She was made with love by a kind and talented chef, who poured the batter into a hot, buttered pan and carefully flipped her over when the time was right.

Patty was happy to be a pancake. She loved the warmth of the griddle, the sizzle of the butter, and the tantalizing aroma of cooking batter. She looked forward to being served to someone special, someone who would appreciate her deliciousness and savor every bite.

But Patty's happiness was short-lived. The chef who made her was overworked and underpaid, and he had too many orders to fill. In his haste, he accidentally burned Patty on one side, leaving a large, unsightly black spot on her otherwise perfect surface.

Patty was devastated. She knew that no one would want to eat a pancake with a burnt spot on it. She felt ashamed and worthless, like she had failed as a pancake. She wished she could disappear, or be magically transformed into something else, anything else, that would make her desirable and loved.

Sure enough, before long, a spatula came along and flipped Patty over onto the other side. But she was no longer the plump, fluffy pancake she had been before. She had lost her moisture, and her texture had become tough and leathery. When the time came for Patty to be served, her human friends took one look at her and frowned. They tried to cut into her, but she was so dry and tough that the knife wouldn't even go through. They tried to choke her down with lots of syrup, but it was no use. Patty was a sad, overcooked pancake, and there was nothing that could be done to save her.

The chef didn't notice the burnt spot on Patty's surface. He simply placed her on a plate, added a dollop of butter and a drizzle of syrup, and sent her out to the dining room. When the server delivered her to a table, the customer took one look at the black spot and pushed her aside, ordering a fresh pancake instead.

Patty was heartbroken. She watched as the other pancakes were cooked and served, each one more perfect than the last. She longed to be one of them, to be enjoyed and appreciated, but she knew it was too late. She had been marked by the chef's mistake, and nothing could change that.

In the end, Patty was never eaten. She sat on the plate, untouched and forgotten, until the end of the day, when she was thrown away with the rest of the uneaten food. She had lived a short, sad life, full of hope and promise, but ultimately ending in disappointment and despair.

> ***"The pancake named Patty certainly experienced feelings of sadness, shame, and worthlessness."***

Patty had been made with love and care, and she had hoped to be enjoyed and appreciated by someone special. But when the chef accidentally burned her, she felt like she had failed as a pancake. She was ashamed of the black spot on her surface, and she knew that no one would want to eat her.

When Patty was eventually rejected by the customer and left untouched on the plate, she felt heartbroken and forgotten. She longed to be appreciated and loved, but she knew that her imperfection had made her unwanted and unlovable. And so, with heavy hearts, Patty's human friends had to throw her away, never to enjoy her delicious goodness again. It was a sad end to a once-happy pancake, and a cautionary tale about the perils of cooking at too high a temperature.

The story of Patty the pancake is a sad one, full of disappointment and despair. It's a reminder that even small mistakes or imperfections can have a big impact on how we see ourselves and how others see us.

Once upon a time, there was a delicious pancake. It was fluffy, golden-brown, and perfect in every way. The pancake had spent its entire life dreaming of being eaten by someone and giving them joy and satisfaction.

One day, the pancake was served on a plate and carried to a table where a hungry customer was waiting. The pancake was excited and proud to be chosen. But as the customer took a bite, they made a face and pushed the plate away. "This pancake is too dry," they said.

The pancake was devastated. It had worked so hard to be the perfect pancake, and now it was rejected. It was left on the plate, uneaten and alone. The hours passed, and the pancake grew cold and stale. Its dreams of being enjoyed by someone were shattered, and it felt useless and forgotten.

Days turned into weeks, and the pancake remained untouched. It was eventually thrown away and left to decompose in a landfill, forgotten by everyone.

The sad story of this pancake is a reminder that even the most well-intentioned efforts can go unappreciated or unrecognized. The pancake wanted nothing more than to bring joy and satisfaction to someone, but instead, it was left to waste away, unwanted and unloved.

Sad Pancake

Mother & Her Seven Children's

ONCE upon a time there was a good housewife, who had seven hungry children. One day she was busy frying pancakes for them, and this time she had used new milk in the making of them. One was lying in the pan, frizzling away -- ah! so beautiful and thick -- it was a pleasure to look at it. The children were standing round the fire, and the husband sat in the corner and looked on.

"Oh, give me a bit of pancake, mother, I am so hungry!" said one child.

"Ah, do! dear mother," said the second.

"Ah, do! dear, good mother," said the third.

"Ah, do! dear, good, kind mother," said the fourth. "Ah, do! dear, good, kind, nice mother," said the fifth. "Ah, do! dear, good, kind, nice, sweet mother," said the sixth.

"Ah, do! dear, good, kind, nice, sweet, darling mother," said the seventh. And thus they were all begging for pancakes, the one more prettily than the other, because they were so hungry, and such good little children.

"Yes, children dear, wait a bit until it turns itself," she answered -- she ought to have said "until I turn it" -- "and then you shall all have pancakes, beautiful pancakes, made of new milk -- only look how thick and happy it lies there."

When the pancake heard this, it got frightened, and all of a sudden, it turned itself and wanted to get out of the pan, but it fell down in it again on the other side, and when it had been fried a little on that side too, it felt a little stronger in the back, jumped out on the floor, and rolled away, like a wheel, right through the door and down the road.

"Halloo!" cried the good wife, and away she ran after it, with the frying pan in one hand and the ladle in the other, as fast as she could, and the children behind her, while the husband came limping after, last of all.

"Halloo, won't you stop? Catch it, stop it. Halloo there!" they all screamed, the one louder than the other, trying to catch it on the run, but the pancake rolled and rolled, and before long, it was so far ahead, that they could not see it, for the pancake was much smarter on its legs than any of them.

When it had rolled a time, it met a man.

"Good day, pancake!" said the man.

"Well met, Manny Panny," said the pancake.

"Dear pancake," said the man, "don't roll so fast, but wait a bit and let me eat you."

"When I have run away from Goody Poody and the husband and seven squalling children, I must run away from you too, Manny Panny," said the pancake, and rolled on and on, until it met a hen.

"Good day, pancake," said the hen.

"Good day, Henny Penny," said the pancake.

"My dear pancake, don't roll so fast, but wait a bit and let me eat you," said the cock.

"When I have run away from Goody Poody and the husband and seven squalling children, and from Manny Panny, I must run away from you too, Henny Penny," said the pancake, and rolled on like a wheel down the road. Then it met a cock.

"My dear pancake, don't roll so fast, but wait a bit and let me eat you," said the duck.

"When I have run away from Goody Poody and the husband and seven squalling children, from Manny Panny, and Henny Penny, I must run away from you too, Cocky Locky," said the pancake, and rolled and rolled on as fast as it could. When it had rolled a long time, it met a duck.

"Good day, pancake," said the duck.

"Good day, Ducky Lucky," said the pancake.

"My dear pancake, don't roll so fast, but wait a bit and let me eat you," said the duck.

"When I have run away from Goody Poody and the husband and seven squalling children, from Manny Panny, and Henny Penny, and Cocky Locky, I must run away from you too, Ducky Lucky," said the pancake, and with that it fell to rolling and rolling as fast as ever it could. When it had rolled a long, long time, it met a goose.

Good day, pancake," said the goose.

"Good day, Goosey Poosey," said the pancake. "My dear pancake, don't roll so fast, but wait a bit and let me eat you," said the goose. "When I have run away from Goody Poody and the husband and seven squalling children, from Manny Panny, and Henny Penny, and Cocky Locky, and Ducky Lucky, I must run away from you too, Goosey Poosey," said the pancake, and away it rolled. So when it had rolled a long, very long time, it met a gander. Good day, pancake," said the gander. "Good day, Gander Pander," said the pancake. "My dear pancake, don't roll so fast, but wait a bit and let me eat you," said the gander. "When I have run away from Goody Poody and the husband and seven squalling children, from Manny Panny, and Henny Penny, and Cocky Locky, and Ducky Lucky, and Goosey Poosey, I must run away from you too, Gander Pander," said the pancake, and rolled and rolled as fast as it could. When it had rolled on a long, long time, it met a pig. Good day, pancake," said the pig. "Good day, Piggy Wiggy," said the pancake, and began to roll on faster than ever. Nay, wait a bit," said the pig, "you needn't be in such a hurry-scurry; we two can walk quietly together and keep each other company through the wood, because they say it isn't very safe there.

" The pancake thought there might be something in that, and so they walked together through the wood; but when they had gone some distance, they came to a brook.

The pig was so fat it wasn't much trouble for him to swim across, but the pancake couldn't get over.

"Sit on my snout," said the pig, "and I will ferry you over."

The pancake did so.

"Ouf, ouf," grunted the pig, and swallowed the pancake in one gulp, and as the pancake couldn't get any farther -- well, you see we can't go on with this story any farther, either.

Hurray

9 798889 860150

Printed by Libri Plureos GmbH in Hamburg,
Germany